BUILDING GUITAR ARRANGEMENTS

FROM THE GROUND UP

BY
MURIEL ANDERSON

 Indicates the audio track number

To access audio visit:
www.halleonard.com/mylibrary

7049-2951-5938-3924

ISBN 978-0-7935-1788-6

7777 W. BLUEMOUND RD. P.O. BOX 13819 MILWAUKEE, WI 53213

Visit Hal Leonard Online at
www.halleonard.com

Muriel Anderson was raised in a musical family in Downers Grove, Illinois. Her mother teaches piano and her grandfather was a saxophone player in John Philip Sousa's band from 1918-1920.

Muriel has performed in almost every musical style, traveling with a bluegrass band, playing in jazz ensembles, touring as a classical guitarist, doing studio work in Nashville, and performing with guitar legend Chet Atkins. She draws from all of these influences to develop a style uniquely her own. In 1989 she became the first woman to win the National Fingerpicking Guitar Championship. She currently records and tours extensively, in halls ranging from Nashville's Grand Ole Opry to Chicago's Orchestra Hall. She teaches at Wheaton College in Illinois and gives workshops for Gibson guitars.

Muriel has released three acclaimed solo CD's / cassettes; *HOMETOWN-Live, ARIOSO FROM PARIS* and *HEARTSTRINGS*. Selections from both *ARIOSO* and *HEARTSTRINGS* have been featured on many airline in-flight programs and in January of 1993 Muriel's *HEARTSTRINGS* cassette traveled 2.5 million miles accompanying the astronauts on a NASA space shuttle mission.

VIDEO

The Building Guitar Arrangements instructional video is available by sending $24.95 to:

Muriel Anderson Video
P.O. Box 168
Elmhurst, IL 60126

Info on concert schedule and recordings is also available at this address.

GROUNDWORK

The first step in finding any melody on the guitar is to become very familiar with the scale and the accompanying chords of the song. This narrows the possibilities of where the melody might lie on the fingerboard. The key of a song is determined by the note upon which the melody comes to rest; usually the last note of the song. Instrumental arrangements can be played in any key, depending on what works best for a particular song.

THEORY: See page 40 for scale construction.

The key of C does not have any sharps or flats and is a convenient key with which to start. Here is the C Major scale (also called simply, the C scale) in first position. Practice moving up and down the scale.

The term "first position" means that the notes on the first fret are to be played with the first (index) finger of the left hand, the notes on the second fret played with the second finger, and the notes on the third fret played with the third finger.

C MAJOR SCALE

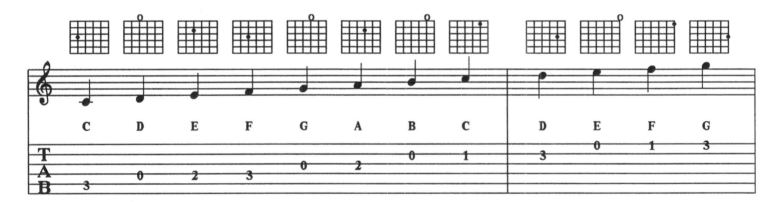

C MAJOR SCALE, CONTINUED

SYNOPSIS: Viewing the C Major scale as a pattern on the fingerboard helps to speed memorization, especially when the notes are played out of sequence. In the diagram below, the "tonic," or first note of the scale is circled. The O's above the diagram mean that those strings may be played open, as notes of the scale.

Notes of the C Major scale in first position:

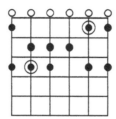

Using the C Major scale diagram as a guide, finger a C Major chord in first position and play the scale again, this time keeping the fingers in the C chord position as much as possible. This is a very important step in building instrumental arrangements.

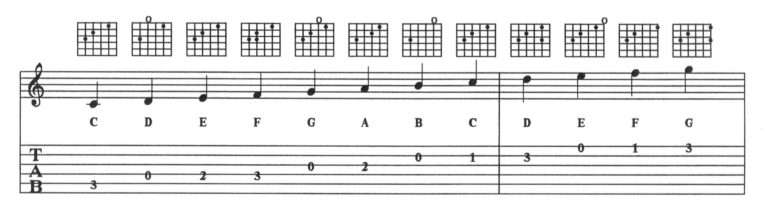

Reminder: The terms "up" and "down," or "up the neck" and "down the neck" always refer to the <u>pitch</u> of the notes, not the physical location on the fingerboard.

TIME SIGNATURES AND NOTE VALUES

Rhythm and timing for a song can usually be figured out by ear, but it may be handy to have a working understanding of how they are notated on a page. The time signature, which looks like a fraction at the beginning of a piece of music is a simple code which indicates how to count the beats in the music, or simply, where to tap your foot.

The bottom number indicates what type of note constitutes a beat. If the bottom number of the fraction is a 4, a quarter note (see diagram on the following page) equals one beat. In other words, you would tap your foot once for each quarter note. If the bottom number is 2, a half note gets one beat. If the bottom number is 8, an eighth note gets one beat.

The top number of the time signature tells you how many beats are in each measure. A measure is defined as the space between two bar lines. The most common time signature is 4/4.

Note values are all relative to one another. The whole note is twice as long as the half note. The half note is twice as long as the quarter note. The quarter note is twice as long as the eighth note. The eighth note is twice as long as the sixteenth note.

In 4/4 time: The *WHOLE NOTE* gets 4 beats, or takes up a whole measure. The *HALF NOTE* gets 2 beats, or takes up half a measure. The *QUARTER NOTE* gets one beat, or takes up 1/4 measure. The *EIGHTH NOTE* gets 1/2 beat, or takes up 1/8 measure. When two or more eighth notes are next to each other, the flag, instead of hanging down (as in the last measure of the examples below), is often drawn connecting the notes. A dot adds half-again the time value of the note.

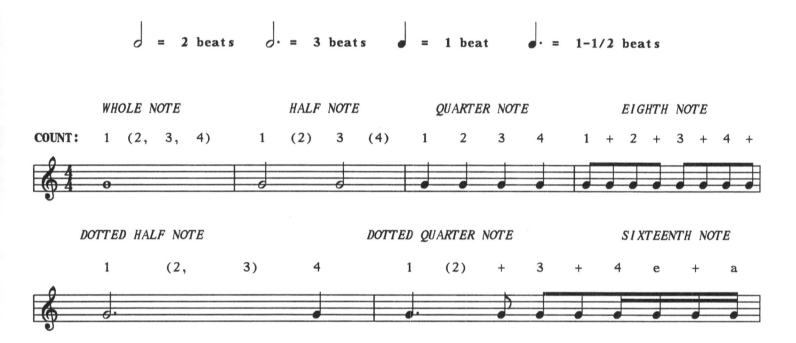

SOUNDING OUT MELODIES

When sounding out a melody by ear, first establish 1) the key of the song (and mode: Major or minor, etc.) and 2) the first note of the song. The key is generally indicated by the last chord, or note, of the song. The first note of the melody is not always the tonic note of the scale. After finding the key, it is always a good idea to run up and down the scale a couple of times. Most of the melody notes will probably be contained in this scale.

When learning from records, you may find it necessary to stop the recording after the first note, hum the note, and find the sound on the guitar. It may be necessary to adjust the tuning of the guitar at this point. Then listen to the next few notes to hear if they are moving up or down the scale (by steps), staying the same, or skipping up or down (by leaps). Hum the notes and find them on the guitar, using the notes of the scale and the chords in that key as a reference.

When sounding out a song from memory, try several keys to see where it sounds best and is easiest to play. If you choose the key of C, for example, first strum a C chord to hear the sound. Sing the first few notes and find them on the guitar, using the diagram of the C Major scale as a reference. Occasionally the melody may use notes outside of the scale. For tips on sounding out chords, see page 41.

For practice, strum a C chord and sound out the first few notes of a familiar melody such as *JINGLE BELLS.* Remember to first sing the melody and listen to whether the notes are moving up or down, by steps of the scale or by leaps.

BEGINNING THE PROCESS OF BUILDING INSTRUMENTALS

Here are the accompanying chords and melody of the Shaker hymn, *SIMPLE GIFTS*. (If you are unfamiliar with standard music notation, use the C Major scale diagrammed on page 4 to help figure out the notes, or you may sound out the melody from the recording. Practice the melody, noting where there is scale movement and where there are skips. Then practice the chord positions.

Next, try playing the melody while keeping the left hand as much as possible in the position of the accompanying chords. The index and pinkie finger of the left hand can catch most of the melody notes while the other two fingers are holding down the bass notes of the chord.

SIMPLE GIFTS

To make an instrumental from this melody line and chords, there are several approaches that can be used, depending on what seems to suit the song best.

I. MELODY ON TOP, BASS NOTES OF THE CHORD ON BOTTOM

Add a bass note from the accompanying chord at the beginning of each measure, and presto! we have a little instrumental. Notice that line 4 is an exact repeat of line two with the exception of the last measure (where the rhythm of the lyrics differs.)

SIMPLE GIFTS
INSTRUMENTAL ARRANGEMENT No. 1

IN GENERAL FOR MELODY-ON-TOP ARRANGEMENTS:

1) If sounding out a melody by ear, find the notes in the top three strings.
2) If the written melody is low in the staff, it must first be transposed up an octave.
3) Also, if the chord changes in the middle of the measure, play the bass note of the new chord on the beat in which the chord change takes place.

II. BLOCK CHORDS

The easiest way to add notes of the chord to the arrangement is with "block" chords (all of the notes played together). At the beginning of each measure, fill in notes of the chord between the melody and bass note. The chords should be played so that the melody note is the highest sounding note of the chord and the bass is the lowest sounding note of the chord. Some or all of the notes in between may be filled in.

SIMPLE GIFTS
INSTRUMENTAL ARRANGEMENT No. 2 WITH BLOCK CHORDS

THE BATTLE HYMN OF THE REPUBLIC is another song that is well suited for a block chord arrangement.

THE BATTLE HYMN OF THE REPUBLIC

When making a block chord arrangement, you will find that sometimes it is more convenient to finger the entire chord and other times just a part of the chord, depending on the preceding notes and the following notes. Try creating an arrangement on your own. Then take a look at the version of the first part on the following page.

Notice that the F or F6 chords can be played with either the 4th string in the bass or the 6th string in the bass. The arrangement builds intensity by waiting until the second half to put the 6th string in the bass. Placing the G in the bass on the C chord in the last line also adds drama by making the C want to lead to the G chord.

THE BATTLE HYMN OF THE REPUBLIC
PART 1 WITH BLOCK CHORDS

10

III. FILLING IN WITH INSIDE VOICES

Often it's nice to start with a very simple arrangement of a song, and then on the second pass through fill it up with some inside voices (play a note or two of the accompanying chord whenever the melody has a held note or rest). Keeping your left hand in the shape of the chord as much as possible makes it easier to play, arrange, and improvise on the arrangement.

SIMPLE GIFTS
ARRANGEMENT No. 3 WITH INSIDE VOICES

* C/E = C chord with E note in the bass

This is just one of many possible arrangements. Improvise by filling in the spaces with different notes of the chord. Not <u>every</u> space needs to be filled in. **Note:** the term "inside voices" is used here because the term "inner voice" implies a counter-melody between the top melody and bass.

The following two arrangements are much more difficult. You may want to give yourself extra time to work on these while you move on to some of the other arrangements.

Take Arrangement #1 of *SIMPLE GIFTS* and experiment with ascending and/or descending bass lines. First, hum the melody and play a scale slowly in the bass, starting with C and moving up or down the scale. The bass notes can be half notes on beats one and three of the measure, or some can be quarter notes to give the arrangement a little more motion. Take the *SIMPLE GIFTS* melody and write in the bass lines that sound best to you. Then practice both parts together slowly, figuring out how to finger the left hand to accommodate both the bass and melody. Sometimes chromatic movement (that is, moving one fret at a time) may be introduced in the bass line to lead from one note to another. Here is one version starting with a descending bass.

SIMPLE GIFTS
INSTRUMENTAL ARRANGEMENT No. 4 WITH WALKING BASS

V. WALKING BASS WITH BLOCK CHORDS

A walking bass may hint at a new set of chords to harmonize a melody. There may be several different chords (containing both the melody note and the bass note) that would work well in a given place in the arrangement.

Here is one possible harmonization of *SIMPLE GIFTS* with a walking bass:

SIMPLE GIFTS
INSTRUMENTAL ARRANGEMENT No.5 WALKING BASS WITH BLOCK CHORDS

VI. ROTATING BASS

⑩

Old-time country-style instrumentals are often composed of a melody and a rotating or alternating bass. The rotating bass is always played with the thumb of the right hand even if the bass goes as high as the third string. **In this book the term "rotating" refers to the thumb moving back and forth between two strings like this:**

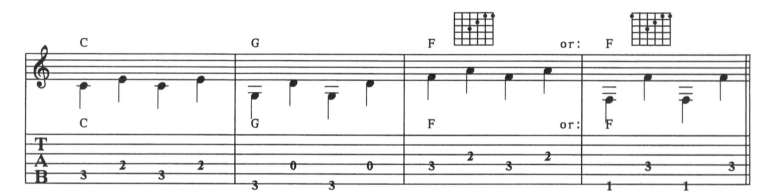

⑪ **EXERCISES**   The following exercises are written with a rotating bass on a C chord. Play each measure (at least) twice as indicated by the repeat signs.

⑭ *Develop the ability to play a melody note on any beat of the measure, while keeping the bass rotating consistently.*

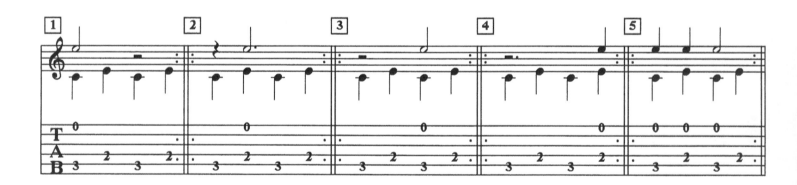

⑫ *Then practice playing a melody note on the off-beats.*

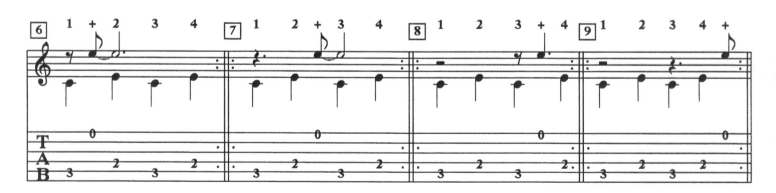

14

Keeping the bass notes of the chord in position, develop the ability to play any desired melody note in the top two strings while keeping the bass rotating consistently. Take these exercises slowly at first.

Rotating bass with C scale Exercise #1:

13
15

Rotating bass with C scale Exercise #2:

These exercises, and others that you may come up with yourself, can help to develop the ability to play any desired note on any beat of the measure while keeping the bass rotating. Then, you are well on your way to arranging and improvising fingerstyle rotating-bass instrumentals. To make an arrangement with rotating bass, play just the bass by itself on the appropriate chord, and hum the melody. Listen to where the melody notes fit in relation to the bass. If working with sheet music, write in the bass notes in each measure. Then play the arrangement very slowly, to get a feel for which melody notes land together with which bass notes. As the speed is gradually increased, listen to make sure that the bass notes are rotating consistently.

A rotating bass for *SIMPLE GIFTS* might look like this:

Or the bass can be played twice as fast, like this:

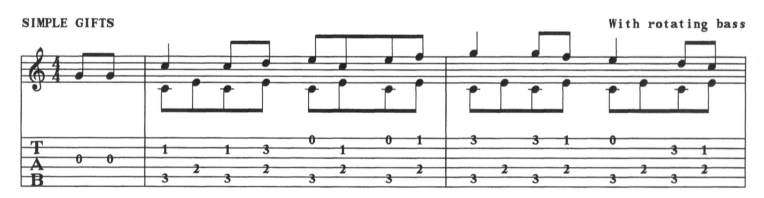

Extended Arrangement:

Mix up the different *SIMPLE GIFTS* instrumentals into one arrangement. For example: Play the first two lines with bass notes at the beginning of each measure [Arr. #1] and the third and fourth lines with block chords [Arr. #2]. Then on the second pass through, play the first two lines with a walking bass [Arr. #4 or #5] and finish by filling in with inside voices [Arr. #3], or a rotating bass version. You may find the rotating bass version of *SIMPLE GIFTS* a little too "busy" for the lyrical melody. Use your own judgement as to which approaches work best for a given song.

Below is the first line of the chorus of *BATTLE HYMN OF THE REPUBLIC* with a rotating bass:

The same approaches, especially the alternating bass technique, can be used with this old-time guitar instrumental made famous by Elizabeth Cotten.

FREIGHT TRAIN

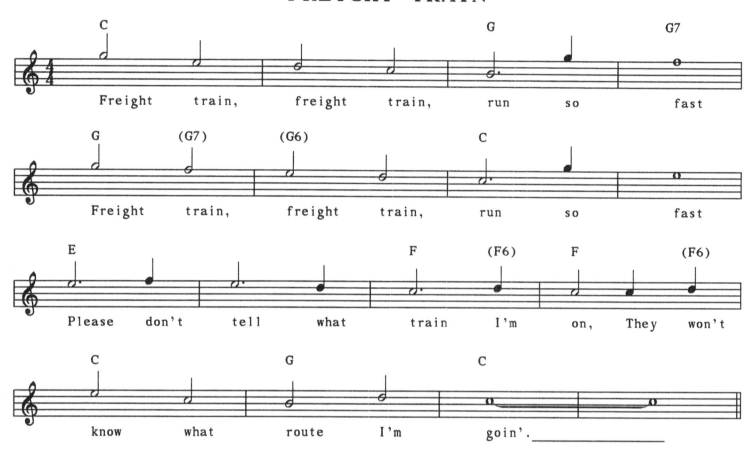

Play the first line of *FREIGHT TRAIN* with a bass note added at the beginning of each measure. Then play the same line rotating between two bass notes of the chord:

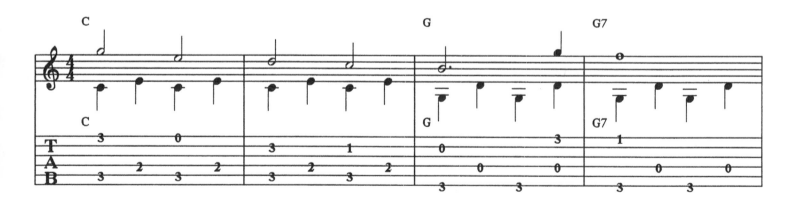

Using this bass pattern, create an arrangement of *FREIGHT TRAIN*. In the version on the following page, the bass run on the last measure returns you to the beginning of the song. For that "Chet Atkins sound," muffle the bass strings lightly very near the bridge, with the side of the palm of your right hand.

FREIGHT TRAIN
ARRANGEMENT No.1 WITH ROTATING BASS

VII. ALTERNATING BASS or Double Rotating Bass

The terms "rotating" and "alternating" are often used interchangeably. However, in this book the term "rotating" refers to the motion of the thumb back and forth between two strings and the term "alternating" refers to the sound of the bass notes going back and forth between the tonic and the fifth (or third) of the chord on beats one and three of the measure. The 5th and 6th strings function as the true bass notes, while the 4th string functions as an in-between note (or chord), much in the same way a honky-tonk pianist plays chords in between the bass notes while the melody is up on top. In fact, guitarist Merle Travis often brushed two or three strings instead of just playing the fourth string to get more of that effect. This type of fingerpicking with a muffled alternating bass is commonly referred to as "Travis-style picking." The motion of the thumb might be described as "double-rotating" like this:

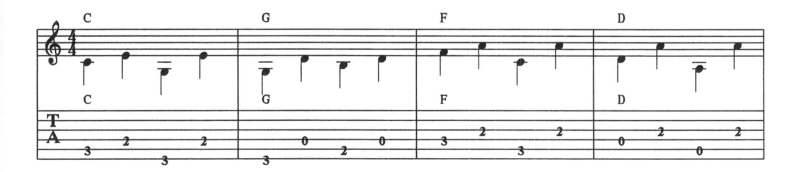

Note that on the C chord the third finger of the left hand must also move back and forth between the 5th string (3rd fret) and the 6th string (3rd fret).

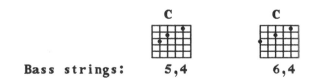

Practice the exercises on page 12 with an alternating, or "double-rotating" bass.

Here is the first line of *SIMPLE GIFTS* with a true alternating bass:

SIMPLE GIFTS
WITH ALTERNATING BASS

Here is *FREIGHT TRAIN* with an alternating bass, but using a single rotating bass for the "F" chord.

FREIGHT TRAIN
ARRANGEMENT No. 2 WITH ALTERNATING BASS

This arrangement is similar to the one recorded by Chet Atkins [RCA Victor #2783, #3558, and 47-8345] and played seemingly by almost every guitar picker in the folk revival of the 60's. Elizabeth Cotten's version [Folkways FG 3526, recorded about 1958] is a little bit different, due in part to the fact that she played the guitar left-handed without restringing it (upside down and backwards from treble to bass).

Instrumental arrangements can grow out of an accompaniment pattern by modifying the right hand pattern and the left hand chord shapes to find the melody notes in the top voice... or enough of the melody to make the song recognizable. (The pattern itself may present ideas for variations in the melody.)

Here are some common fingerpicking patterns (on the C chord):

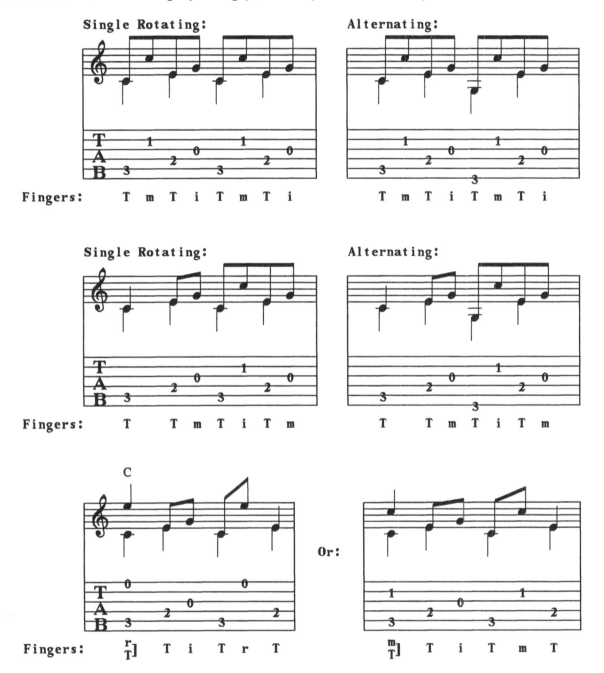

(T=thumb, i=index, m=middle, r=ring)

The last pair of patterns work very well for *FREIGHT TRAIN*. Practice the pattern by itself until you can play it in your sleep before working it into an instrumental arrangement. Depending on where the melody is located, the second string may be played instead of the first string. Also, depending on the chord, the 6th string may be played in the bass instead of the 5th string.

On the following page is a version with single rotating bass. The same arrangement can be played with an alternating, or double rotating bass.

FREIGHT TRAIN
ARRANGEMENT No.3 WITH FINGERPICKING PATTERN

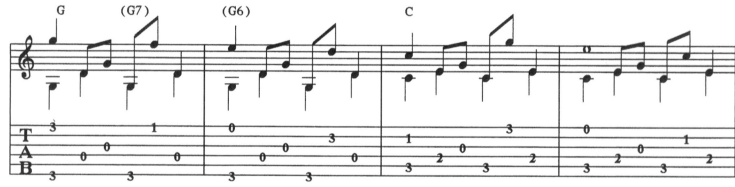

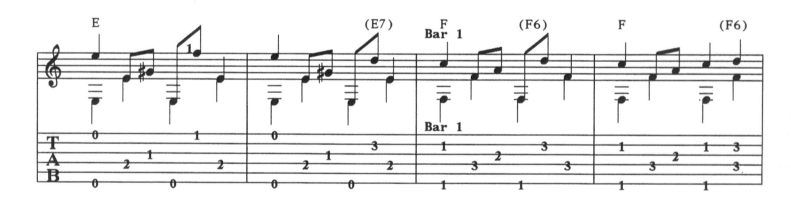

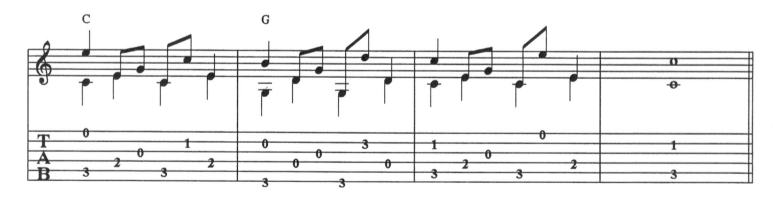

IX. SYNCOPATION

The version of *FREIGHT TRAIN* with a fingerpicking pattern naturally syncopates the melody by placing some of the melody notes between the beats. Try playing a simple rotating bass, placing some of the melody notes before or after the beat. Here is one example. There are many possible ways to syncopate a melody.

FREIGHT TRAIN
ARRANGEMENT No.4 WITH SYNCOPATED MELODY

ON YOUR OWN: Make an extended arrangement of *FREIGHT TRAIN* starting with the bare melody harmonized by block chords and a walking bass; more or less like a church hymn. Then go to a lively alternating bass.

X. MELODY IN THE BASS

Instrumentals can be built with the melody in the bass and the chords on top. The bass melody may be played with a flatpick or the thumb of the right hand, and the higher strings of the chord strummed whenever there is enough time. A classic example of a bass-melody instrumental is this old Appalachian song. Mother Maybelle and the Carter Family did a version that became popular with folk guitarists across the country.

WILDWOOD FLOWER

I will twine, I will min – gle my wa – ving black hair with the ro- ses so red and the li- li es so fair, and the myr- tle so green with an em- er- ald hue, the pale e- man – ita and__ vio- lets so blue.

When playing *WILDWOOD FLOWER* the chords can be strummed whenever there is a half note in the melody. In general, only the top three strings, or the notes above the melody note, are strummed. Full chords may be fingered throughout the song, but it is sometimes better to leave some fingers off when they are not needed. (For example the bass notes on the G7 chords.) Try it on your own, then take a look at the arrangement on the following page.

To give melody-in-bass arrangements a little more motion, try strumming down-up with the fingers or the pick, instead of a straight down-stroke. For a more fluid, "Country" feel, the down-stroke gets more emphasis, and the up-stroke is more like a light pick-up to the following bass note. In tablature, it would look like this:

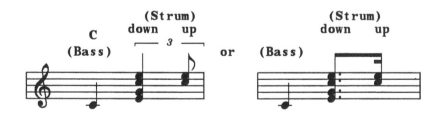

24

WILDWOOD FLOWER
WITH MELODY IN THE BASS

ON YOUR OWN: Sound out the melody of *SIMPLE GIFTS* an octave lower. Then look at the arrangement on the following page.

FILLING IN SPACE

When there is extra space to fill (a held or dotted note, or a rest) either an extra bass note or an extra strum can be added. The slashes in the standard notation (top stave) represent strums on the chords indicated above.

SIMPLE GIFTS
WITH MELODY IN BASS

ON YOUR OWN: Here are the first lines of several melodies. Complete melody-in-the-bass arrangements of the following songs. The slashes indicate strums.

FREIGHT TRAIN

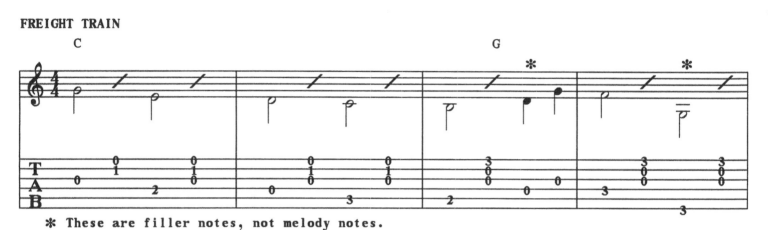

* These are filler notes, not melody notes.

HOME ON THE RANGE

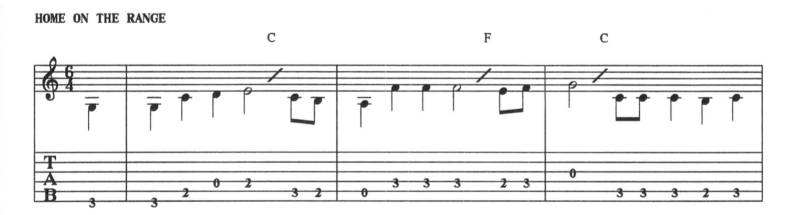

IRENE GOOD NIGHT

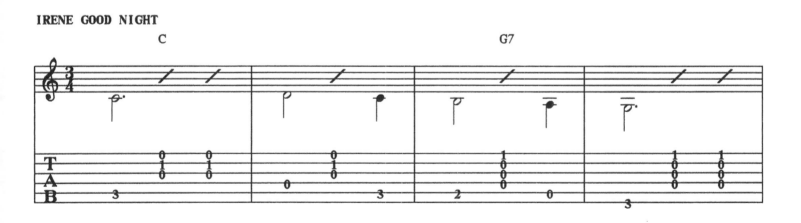

XI. 3/4 TIME; KEY OF G

Practice the G Major scale thoroughly before starting on the following instrumental. Below is a diagram of all the notes in first position in the G Major scale. Notice that it is identical to the C Major scale except that all the "F" notes are raised one fret to "F♯." The "G's" or tonic notes are double circles. Always start and end on one of these notes when practicing the scale.

Here is the first line of *SIMPLE GIFTS* in the key of G. Notice that the interval relationships (scalar movement and skips) are the same as in the original key. The sharp at the beginning of the staff indicates that all the F's are to be sharped unless canceled by a natural sign.

Here are the first three lines of *TAKE ME OUT TO THE BALL GAME*. Find the rest of the melody and chords by ear before looking at the instrumental arrangement. There are two notes that go outside of the scale. (D♯ and C♯ notes in measures 9 and 28.)

TAKE ME OUT TO THE BALL GAME

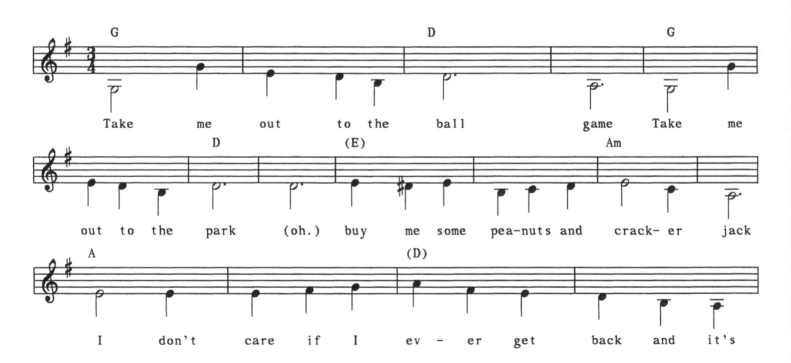

Chords used in *TAKE ME OUT TO THE BALL GAME*: G, D, E, Am, A7, (C♯o), C. For tips on sounding out chords, see page 41. In the arrangement on the following page, the slashes represent strums (on the chord indicated above the slash).

TAKE ME OUT TO THE BALL GAME

XII. ARPEGGIOS

One type of pattern picking is the arpeggio; notes of a chord played one at a time in sequence from high to low or low to high, etc. Many slower songs are often accompanied by an arpeggio. This arpeggio can be used as the basis for an instrumental. However, on some songs it may be difficult to keep the accompaniment from getting in the way of the melody. As in other pattern picking arrangements, the arpeggio may have to be altered significantly to accomodate the melody. An arpeggio can be used in a melody-in-the-bass arrangement simply by replacing the strum with a short arpeggio pattern.

Here are some common arpeggio patterns (on the C chord):

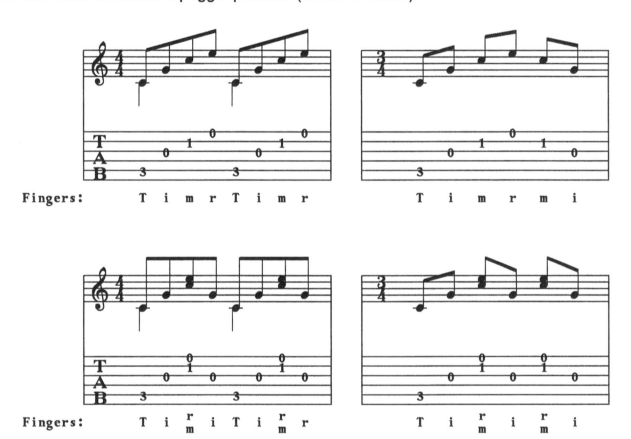

The song *HOUSE OF THE RISING SUN* uses the second pattern. It is possible to create an instrumental arrangement by replacing certain notes of the arpeggio with the melody notes that fall on those beats. The rest of the accompaniment notes should be altered (if neccesary) so that they are not the same as the melody note in close proximity.

Often the melody will cross over from the bottom voice to a middle voice or an upper voice. It is especially important then to play the melody notes <u>louder</u> than the accompaniment notes.

HOUSE OF THE RISING SUN is an example of a song in a minor key. The melody comes to rest on the Am chord. The E chord at the last measure is a turn-around to get into the next verse; the song will actually end on an Am. Also notice the occasional use of G♯'s. It is common in minor keys to sharp the 7th note of the scale (called the *harmonic minor*, see page 40.)

In 6/8 time you will find the same number of eighth notes per measure as 3/4 time. The difference is in the accent, or pulse. In a measure with six eighth notes, for instance, in 3/4 time the accent is on every other note to give 3 beats per measure, and in 6/8 time the accent is on every third note to give 2 beats per measure. Or a very slow 6/8 time may have a pulse on each eighth note to give 6 beats per measure.

HOUSE OF THE RISING SUN

TRANSPOSING

Transposing is often necessary because a song may sound better or finger easier in one key than another. Or, when accompanying voice, it may be easier to sing in one key than another. If working from sheet music, the best key is rarely the one in which the song is written. Also, a modulation to a different key is a nice way to lengthen an arrangement. Transposing is simply the process of moving all the chords and all the notes up (or down) the same interval. The easiest way is to move everything the same number of scale degrees and impose the new key signature. For example:

Example #1
Original key: C ---- transpose to: D (move everything up one whole step)
The key of D has two sharps (F♯ and C♯). Notice that when a note or chord is sharped or flatted (C♯°), it is also done in the new key (D♯°).

Original key:	C,	F,	G7,	C,	Em7,	C♯°,	Dm,	G7,	C
Transposed to D:	D,	G,	A7,	D,	F♯m7,		D♯°,	Em,	A7,D

Example #2
Original key: C ---- transpose to: G (up a 5th, or up 4 notes in the scale)
Move everything up 4 notes in the scale. Since the key of G has one sharp (F♯) all the F's in the new key become F♯'s.

Original key:	C,	F,	G7,	B7,	E7,	Am,	Dm,	G7,	C
Transposed to G:	G,	C,	D7,	F♯7,	B7,	Em,	Am,	D7,	G

FINDING THE KEY SIGNATURE USING THE CIRCLE OF FIFTHS

The new key signature can be found easily by referring to the circle of fifths, which you can draw by starting with a C note and writing the note which is a fifth higher to its right, progressing around clockwise until you return to C. The sharps and flats fall into a neat pattern, always following the same order. The right hand side of the circle contains the sharp keys. The key of C has no sharps (or flats), the key of G has one sharp, the key of D has two sharps, etc. The left hand side of the circle contains the flat keys. The key of F has one flat, the key of B♭ has two flats, etc.

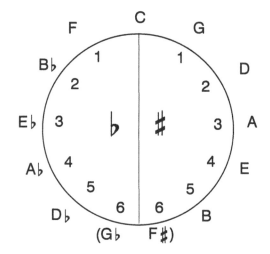

ORDER OF SHARPS: F♯, C♯, G♯, D♯, A♯, (E♯, B♯)
If there is one sharp in the key, it is F♯. If there are two sharps, they are F♯ and C♯. If there are three sharps, they are F♯, C♯ and G♯, etc.

ORDER OF FLATS: B♭, E♭, A♭, D♭, G♭, (C♭, F♭)
If there is one flat, it is B♭. If there are two flats, B♭ and E♭, etc.

(Reminder: a sharp raises the pitch one fret; a flat lowers the pitch one fret. Every sharp note also has a flat name, and vice versa. G♭=F♯ (as indicated) and D♭=C♯, A♭=G♯, etc.]

XII. DROPPED TUNINGS

DROPPED D TUNING

When playing in the key of D, it is often effective to lower, or loosen, the 6th string a whole step to a D note. The 6th string will then be an octave lower than the 4th string. With this new tuning it is possible to play the 6th and 5th strings open while playing a melody over a D chord. Remember that fretted notes on the 6th string are now located two frets higher than in standard tuning. For example, the G bass is on the 5th fret, and low E is on the second fret. Here are some chord diagrams using a dropped D tuning. The x's over the strings mean not to play those strings, and o's are above the strings that may be played open.

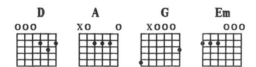

ON YOUR OWN: Here is the first line of *SIMPLE GIFTS* in the key of D. Make an arrangement using dropped D tuning.

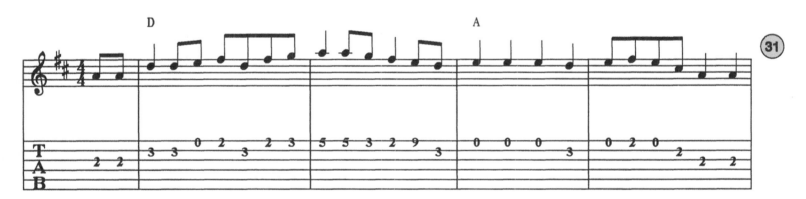

DROPPED G TUNING

When playing in the key of G, it is often effective to lower both the 6th string a whole step to a D note, and the 5th string to a G note. This makes it easier to play a melody with G bass notes (open in the 6th and 5th strings) and the low bass notes give the arrangement an "open tuning" sound. Remember that fretted notes on the 6th and 5th strings are now located two frets higher than in standard tuning. For example, the C note on the 5th string is on the 5th fret. Below are some chord diagrams using a dropped G tuning.

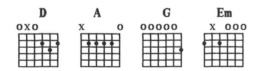

Look at the first line of *SIMPLE GIFTS* in the key of G on page 28. Make an arrangement which uses G tuning. Then look at the version on page 42.

FINDING CHORDS UP THE NECK

It is important to be able to find chords in all positions on the guitar, especially when notes of the melody are pitched high, or if it is more convenient to play the notes from an upper position chord. Taking the chords up the neck can make it possible to play the melody an octave higher. It can also provide an almost instant harmony part, or provide ideas for variations on the melody.

Review Major chord positions. (Refer to the book CHORD CONSTELLATIONS pages 6-7.) The same series of shapes is used for all major chords. Any chord shape can be moved so that scale degree (1), which identifies the name of the chord, falls on the tonic note of the desired chord.

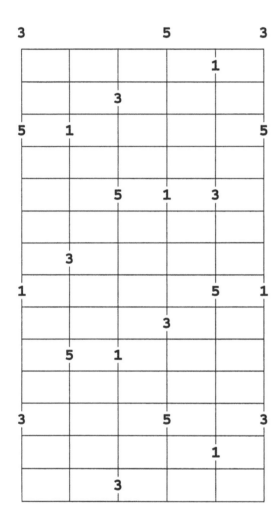

Examine this part of the Major chord diagram. (You may recognize it in this position as a D chord.) These numbers refer to the <u>scale degrees</u>, not the fingering.

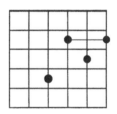

Scale degrees: 3 5 1 3

Move this position up the neck to form a G Major chord. The scale degree (1) should fall on the G note, or 8th fret, 2nd string. Then of course, the (5) and the (3) on the first and third strings fall on the seventh fret and the (3) on the fourth string falls on the ninth fret.

Bar the first three strings with the index finger. Most of the melody notes of *SIMPLE GIFTS* in G (an octave higher) are located right in this position and dropped G tuning will provide the bass notes in the 5th and 6th strings. Sound out the melody by ear starting with scale degrees 5-5-1. Now look at the arrangement on page 44.

ON YOUR OWN: Use this position for a G chord. Also find a C chord up the neck on the top four strings, using a different shape. [Tonic (1) is on the 8th fret, first string.] With these two chords (no bass notes) improvise a harmony part to *SIMPLE GIFTS*. This can be done using a simple fingerpicking pattern, or the fourth finger of the left hand can also be used to find some extra harmony notes convenient to the chord shapes.

THIRDS

Following the melody in thirds can add a nice effect to an arrangement. Practice playing a C Major scale harmonized in thirds:

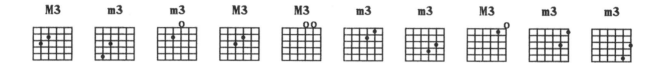

Each of the resulting intervals can be either a minor third (m3 = the interval of three half-steps] or a Major third [M3 = the interval of four half-steps.] Notice that the shapes are different on the second and third strings than on the other pairs of strings, due to the fact that the strings are tuned to a different interval.

Harmony can be added above or below the melody. Play a section of *SIMPLE GIFTS* with notes of the scale a third below the melody.

*Sometimes the interval of a fourth can also be used, as in the above example, when it falls on a note of the chord.

SIXTHS

Following a melody in sixths (with an occasional fifth) can be approached in the same way as in thirds (with an occasional fourth).

Practice a scale harmonized in sixths.

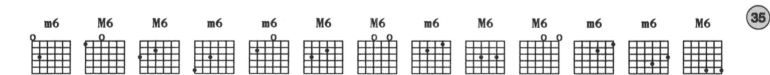

ON YOUR OWN: Play a section of *SIMPLE GIFTS* with harmony notes a sixth below the melody. An occasional fifth may also be used.

HAMMER-ONS, PULL-OFFS, AND SLIDES

Hammer-ons and pull-offs are very common techniques, both to make two notes legato (indicated in musical notation as a slur, or curved line) and to ornament a melody or accompaniment note.

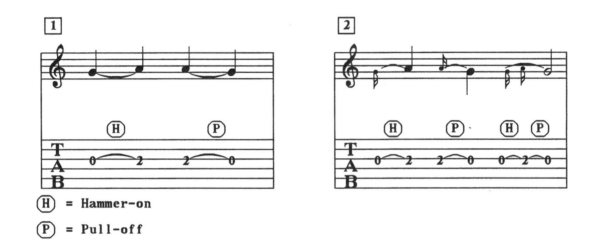

(H) = Hammer-on

(P) = Pull-off

A hammer-on (or as classical players will call it, an ascending slur) is accomplished by striking the string once with the right hand and hammering the left hand finger onto the next note with enough force so that the note will sound without striking again with the right hand. Staying on the tips of the fingers, close to the frets, will help make clearer hammer-ons.

We touched on pull-offs in the *WILDWOOD FLOWER* arrangement. A pull-off (or descending slur) is accomplished by striking a fretted note and instead of simply lifting the finger to reveal the next note, pulling the left hand finger downward so that the next note will sound without being struck again with the right hand.

A slide is another way to connect two notes on the same string. It is indicated in musical notation by a straight line leading from one note to the next.

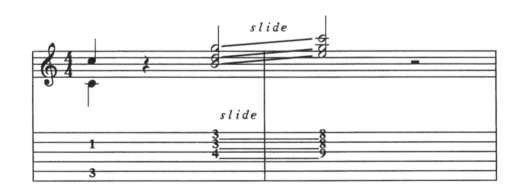

Slides, hammer-ons and pull-offs are used in the following elaborated version of *WILDWOOD FLOWER*.

WILDWOOD FLOWER

There are many ways to begin and end arrangements other than simply starting at the top and ending with the last note of the melody. On the following page are several approaches, although there is much room for originality in both intros and endings.

INTROS AND ENDINGS

1. The last line, or last phrase of the song can be used as an introduction.   In any of the *SIMPLE GIFTS* arrangements, you might start at the third measure from the end, fourth beat (last two notes) of the measure.   Or, you could start five measures from the end on the last beat of the measure.   In the *FREIGHT TRAIN* arrangements, you could start five measures from the end, third beat (last two notes) of the measure.   You could also start eight measures from the end, on the first beat of the measure.   This leads smoothly into the beginning of the song.

2. Play the melody slowly and free-form as a solo line or with chordal accompaniment before going into the arrangement in time.

3. Play a bass run which leads into the beginning of the arrangement.

4. Use part of the melody in a sequence to create a riff which ends on the V chord (see page 41) of the first chord in the arrangement.   Or play a riff which goes into a bass run leading back to the beginning.

5. Begin with part of a scale, arpeggio passage, or a descending chromatic riff which ends on the V chord of the first chord in the arrangement. The following is a descending chromatic riff borrowed from a ragtime fingerstyle tune called *ALL THUMBS* by Mark Casstevens. It is adapted to work as an intro to *FREIGHT TRAIN.*

FREIGHT TRAIN   Introduction

Some of the very same techniques can be used for endings.

1. Repeat the last line. You may want to slow down gradually at the end (ritard) or leave a little more time just before the last note.

2. Play part of a scale, arpeggio passage, or chromatic riff which stays in character with the arrangement. Here is an ending to *FREIGHT TRAIN* which replaces the last two measures. This is a very common ending which uses the interval of a sixth, descending chromatically.

A very effective and more difficult way to arrange a piece for guitar is to take a recording or sheet music for a piece usually played on other instruments and find the same notes on the guitar. Using the thumb to play the bass line and fingers to play the melody, the guitar may have the capability of handling two or three parts at once.

In *NOLA*, open strings are interspersed with fretted notes to give a harplike sound. Here are the first few lines:

SCALE CONSTRUCTION

THE MAJOR SCALE:
Most songs that we know are based upon the Major or minor scale. The Major scale is a simple formula of half steps (the distance of one fret) and whole steps (the distance of two frets). The sequence from one note to the next is:

STARTING NOTE - *whole step - whole step - half step - whole step - whole step - whole step - half step*

MAJOR

The formula can be thought of as two groups of whole-whole-half, separated be a whole step. The first note of the scale is also the name of the scale, called the "tonic" or "root." For example, the E Major scale uses the same sequence of whole steps and half steps, but starts on an E note. You will notice that some of the notes fall on sharps, in particular: F♯, C♯, G♯ and D♯, which explains why these notes are sharped in the E Major scale. However, the F Major scale contains no sharps, but one flat: B♭. (We choose to call this note a B♭ rather than A♯ so that we have one of each letter name in the scale.)

THE MINOR SCALE:
The natural minor scale uses the same series of whole and half steps, but starts on the sixth note of the Major scale sequence. This shifts the whole and half step sequence to:

STARTING NOTE - *whole step - half step - whole step - whole step - half step - whole step - whole step*

NATURAL MINOR   HARMONIC MINOR

MELODIC MINOR

Because the half steps and whole steps fall in different places, the 3rd, 6th, and 7th notes of the natural minor scale are a half step lower than in the Major scale. There are two other varieties of the minor scale that are used frequently. one is called the *harmonic minor*. In the harmonic minor scale the 7th note, or 7th degree of the minor scale is raised a half step. Another variation is called the *melodic minor*. In the melodic minor, the 6th and 7th degrees of the minor scale are raised a half step (to sound more like the Major scale) when the notes are ascending, and they revert back to the natural minor when the notes are descending.

SOUNDING OUT CHORDS AND THE HARMONIZED SCALE

Many of the melody notes are contained in the chords of a song. Likewise, the important melody notes are clues to the accompanying chords. Knowing a little about chords that most often occur in a given key can help speed up the process of finding them by ear. When sounding out a chord from a recording, listen for and sing the top note of the chord, the bottom note of the chord, and then try to sing some of the notes in between, to see if they match the sound of the chord. Then find those notes on the guitar.

Chords that often occur in a given key can be found by using the "Harmonized Scale." Chords can be built upon each of the notes of the scale by stacking up thirds upon each of the notes of the scale. (A "third" is the interval between the first and third note of the scale, or the second and fourth note of the scale, etc.) The resultant chords will be the ones that occur naturally (without using any sharps or flats) in the key.

Chords built upon scale degrees are often referred to by Roman numerals. The I, IV, and V chords in any key will always be Major. These are the most common chords in Western music. Remember always to count the tonic (the name of the scale, or "root") as "1." The V chord is often found as a dominant seventh, or V7. In the key of C the I, IV and V chords would be C, F, and G (or V7=G7). Among these three basic chords are contained all of the seven notes of the scale. The ii, iii, and iv chords in any key will always be minor (often indicated by lower case Roman numerals or a minus [-] sign). The vii chord (rarely used) is a diminished triad (triad=chord with three notes).

The harmonized scale can be expanded (add another third to the top of each chord) to create all the <u>seventh</u> chords that occur naturally within a key. The result is: I7=Major seventh, ii7=minor seventh, iii7=minor seventh, IV7=Major seventh, V7=Dominant seventh, vi7=minor seventh, vii7=half-diminished seventh, or minor seventh flat-five. In the key of C: CM7, Dm7, Em7, FM7, G7, Am7, Bm7-5. The most common seventh chord is the V7 or dominant seventh. In the key of C this would be G7.

COMMON PROGRESSIONS

Some common chord progressions (using Roman numerals) are:

V - I
IV - V - I
I - IV - I - V - I
I - VI - II - V - I

Play these progressions in the key of C. Then play them substituting V7 for V (G7 for G). You have probably heard these chord changes in many songs.

It should be noted that in many songs, chords may be borrowed from other keys. The most common diversion from the harmonized scale is using the Major or Dominant 7th chord built upon the 5th degree of another chord. This creates a momentary V - I progression in a new key. For example, the V chord of G is D Major. So the chords D-G-C form the very common progression II-V-I with the II Major instead of minor (borrowed from the key of G.)

SIMPLE GIFTS FINAL ARRANGEMENT
(Transcription from "HEARTSTRINGS" cassette/CD, Muriel Anderson)

SIMPLE GIFTS

Shaker Spiritul
Arr. Muriel Anderson

6th – D
5th – G

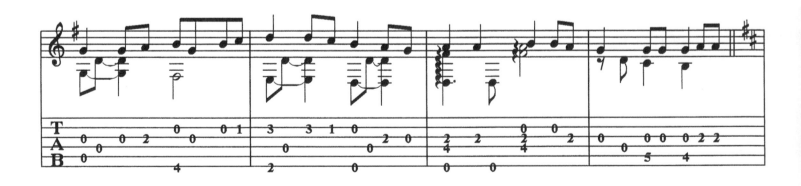

44

There are many guitar techniques that can be used as integral parts of an arrangement. When in the final stages of your arranging, keep in mind as many right hand and left hand techniques as you can, and play with the possibilities.

ON YOUR OWN: Make an extended arrangement of a familiar song such as *JINGLE BELLS* using some or all of the following techniques:

♪ - Melody on top, bass note at the beginning of each measure

♪ - Block chords

♪ - Filling in with inside voices

♪ - Walking Bass

♪ - Rotating bass or alternating bass

♪ - Pattern picking, arpeggio or syncopated melody

♪ - Melody in bass

♪ - Modulate to G

♪ - Up the neck, an octave higher

♪ - Harmonize some parts in thirds or sixths

This is by no means the end of the process of building guitar arrangements; it is merely a beginning point. As in any creative process, be open to the fact that there will be some things in your arranging that are not explained here, or that may not have explanations at all - they just sound good.

Graphics by Paul Kurtz

Special thanks to Kathy Tyers, John Knowles, and Guy Van Duser for their assistance.

SIMPLE GIFTS

'Tis the gift to be simple, 'tis the gift to be free
'Tis the gift to come down where we ought to be
And when we find ourselves in the place just right
It will be in the valley of love and delight

Chorus:
When true simplicity is gained
To bow and to bend we will not be ashamed
To turn, to turn will be our delight
'Till by turning, turning we come round right

'Tis the gift to be gentle, 'tis the gift to be fair
'Tis the gift to wake and breathe the morning air
To walk every day in the path that we choose
'Tis a gift we pray we may never, never lose

'Tis the gift to be knowing, 'tis the gift to be kind
'tis the gift to wait and hear another's mind
That when we speak our feelings we might come out true
'Tis a gift for me and a gift for you

'Tis the gift to be loving, 'tis the best gift of all
Like a warm spring rain bringing beauty when it falls
And when we use this gift we may come to believe
It is better to give than it is to receive

TEACH YOURSELF TO PLAY
GUITAR SONGS

Teach yourself to play your favorite songs on guitar with this multi-media learning experience! Each song in each book includes a comprehensive online video lesson with an interactive song transcription, slow-down features, looping capabilities, track choices, play-along functions, and more. The price of the books includes access to all of these online features!

"COME AS YOU ARE" & 9 MORE ROCK HITS

Come As You Are (Nirvana) • Do I Wanna Know? (Artic Monkeys) • Heaven (Los Lonely Boys) • Here Without You (3 Doors Down) • Learn to Fly (Foo Fighters) • Plush (Stone Temple Pilots) • Santeria (Sublime) • Say It Ain't So (Weezer) • 21 Guns (Green Day) • Under the Bridge (Red Hot Chili Peppers).

Book with Online Audio & Video
00152224 .... $17.99

"MORE THAN WORDS" & 9 MORE ACOUSTIC HITS

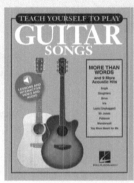

Angie (The Rolling Stones) • Daughters (John Mayer) • Drive (Incubus) • Iris (Goo Goo Dolls) • Layla (Eric Clapton) • Mr. Jones (Counting Crows) • More Than Words (Extreme) • Patience (Guns N' Roses) • Wonderwall (Oasis) • You Were Meant for Me (Jewel).

Book with Online Audio & Video
00152225 .... $17.99

"CROSSROADS" & 9 MORE BLUES CLASSICS

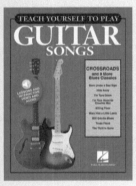

Born Under a Bad Sign Albert King) • Cross Road Blues (Crossroads) (Cream) • Hide Away (Freddie King) • I'm Tore Down (Eric Clapton) • I'm Your Hoochie Coochie Man (Muddy Waters) • Killing Floor (Howlin' Wolf) • Mary Had a Little Lamb (Buddy Guy) • Still Got the Blues (Gary Moore) • Texas Flood (Stevie Ray Vaughan and Double Trouble) • The Thrill Is Gone (B.B. King).

Book with Online Audio & Video
00152183 .... $17.99

"SMOKE ON THE WATER" & 9 MORE HARD ROCK CLASSICS

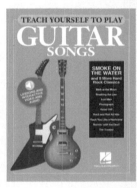

Bark at the Moon (Ozzy Osbourne) • Breaking the Law (Judas Priest) • Iron Man (Black Sabbath) • Photograph (Def Leppard) • Rebel Yell (Billy Idol) • Rock and Roll All Nite (KISS) • Rock You like a Hurricane (Scorpions) • Runnin' with the Devil (Van Halen) • Smoke on the Water (Deep Purple) • The Trooper (Iron Maiden).

Book with Online Audio & Video
00152230 .... $17.99

"DUST IN THE WIND" & 9 MORE FINGERPICKING CLASSICS

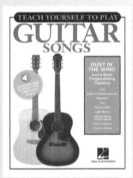

Anji (Simon & Garfunkel) • Babe, I'm Gonna Leave You (Led Zeppelin) • Blackbird (The Beatles) • Dee (Randy Rhoads) • Dust in the Wind (Kansas) • Fire and Rain (James Taylor) • Little Martha (The Allman Brothers Band) • Take Me Home, Country Roads (John Denver) • Tears in Heaven (Eric Clapton) • Time in a Bottle (Jim Croce).

Book with Online Audio & Video
00152184 .... $17.99

"SWEET HOME ALABAMA" & 9 MORE ROCK CLASSICS

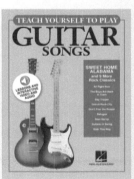

All Right Now (Free) • The Boys Are Back in Town (Thin Lizzy) • Day Tripper (The Beatles) • Detroit Rock City (KISS) • Don't Fear the Reaper (Blue Oyster Cult) • Refugee (Tom Petty and the Heartbreakers) • Start Me Up (The Rolling Stones) • Sultans of Swing (Dire Straits) • Sweet Home Alabama (Lynyrd Skynyrd) • Walk This Way (Aerosmith).

Book with Online Audio & Video
00152181 .... $17.99

Each song includes online video lesson!

HAL•LEONARD®
CORPORATION
7777 W. Bluemound Rd. P.O. Box 13819 Milwaukee, WI 53213

www.halleonard.com

Prices, content and availability subject to change without notice.

0516

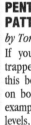
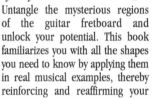

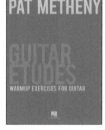
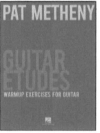

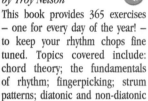

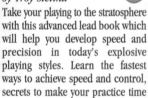